The Big Book of Positive Affirmations for Black Kids
-2 Books in 1-

Positive Affirmations for Black Kids

Positive Affirmations for Black Kids Volume 2

Nia Simone

Contents

Positive Affirmations for Black Kids

Thoughtful Affirmations Designed to
Increase Self-Confidence, Instill Self-Esteem,
Grow Resilience, and Encourage Self-Love

Nia Simone

Contents

Introduction

In an age where society is becoming increasingly aware of the power of words and their profound influence on our brains and self-concept, the importance of nurturing our self-worth and self-esteem has never been more paramount. This is especially true for children. Growing up in a world where we are constantly reminded of our color, Black kids face challenges that their peers might not always understand. Systemic prejudices that persist can cast shadows on their dreams and aspirations and end up having a negative impact on their self-esteem. So it is imperative to realize the transformative power of positive self-talk and positive affirmations.

Our thoughts, our words, and our inner dialogue are very powerful. So powerful, that they can and do change our self-perception and the pathways in our brains. There is now scientific evidence that our thoughts and words, both positive and negative, impact our mental well-being, change our brain's pathways, and change how we think. Think about that for a second; our thoughts and words physically change our brains. That is incredible. Incredibly powerful. Let's make sure to teach our kids to hold positive thoughts.

This knowledge is a fantastic tool that is should we decide to use it. So let's use it! Let's use this to our advantage and to the benefit of our children. Growing up is hard, growing up black is harder, and growing up in this post-pandemic world is harder still.

Recent insights into positive psychology have shed light on the intricate relationship between the repetition of positive affirmations and resulting changes in the neural pathways in our brains. The consistent repetition of specific thoughts, especially positive affirmations, can change the brain, cells, and genes. By constantly reinforcing positive affirmations, individuals are rewiring their thought processes. This is amazing; and game-changing. Let's give this to our kids and encourage them to use it to feel better about themselves and boost their confidence.

Our internal dialogue or "self-talk" plays in our minds throughout the day is a mixture of both empowering and limiting beliefs. Positive affirmations, or structured "self-talk," are countermeasures against fear-based or self-sabotaging thoughts. Think of these positive affirmations as exercises for our mind and brain. Just as physical exercises fortify our bodies, positive affirmations are repetitive mental exercises that strengthen our cognitive faculties.

By practicing them, we engage in a process of "reprogramming" our brain, eliminating pain pathways (physical or psychological) and replacing them with new, constructive, affirming thoughts.

Positive Affirmations for Black Kids is an essential toolkit designed to empower black children with a strong sense of self-worth, confidence, and cultural identity. It is more than just a book of affirmations; it is an actionable tool designed to make our kids feel good about themselves, confident in their abilities, and aware of their value and place in this world. It emphasizes the undeniable power of words to shape minds; especially young and impressionable ones. When chosen thoughtfully, words can be a robust shield against the world's negative influences and reinforce a child's belief in themselves.

Please say each affirmation aloud, in your mind, or write it down; whatever works best for you. The goal is to feel each affirmation and internalize it. It is my recommendation that you read (and repeat) these affirmations as part of your daily routine. If possible, 5-10 minutes in the morning and 5-10 minutes in the evening before bed is ideal.

Affirmations

It is a great day to feel empowered and take advantage of every opportunity.

♥

I have the power to do anything I set my mind to. I have a great start to the day.

♥

I have a purpose. I belong in this world. I want to explore and achieve great things.

♥

I am filled with hope.

♥

I am intelligent.

♥

I can set my mind to do anything I want.

♥

I have self-worth and can accomplish anything I set my mind to.

♥

I am confident and unique, and I can perform better at school.

♥

I have value, and I have meaning in this world. I matter to the world, and I can give back.

♥

The people who deserve to love me will be excited to accept the real me.

♥

I am resilient; no one can tear me down.

♥

I am thoughtful and considerate.

♥

I believe in myself.

♥

I am healthy and happy.

♥

I am full of great ideas and thoughts.

♥

I have the power to create anything I desire.

♥

I am unique and special. I have the confidence to be myself.

♥

My life is fun and filled with joy.

♥

I am proud of the person I am becoming.

♥

I deserve good things to happen in my life.

♥

I am a fast learner.

♥

I love to learn new things. I make learning fun and creative.

♥

I am enough and do not have to change myself to be enough.

♥

I have unlimited potential within me. I have many talents.

♥

I am wonderful, just as I am.

♥

I feel happy and excited to experience each day.

♥

I am destined for greatness, and I believe in my journey.

♥

Every day is a new chance to shine brighter.

♥

I come from a rich Black heritage that empowers me.

♥

I look good today.

♥

I speak to myself with kindness.

♥

I am kind, and thoughtful, and my presence makes a difference.

♥

My creativity knows no bounds.

♥

I trust in my abilities and the decisions I make.

♥

My confidence inspires others around me.

♥

I am magical, and my essence is enchanting.

♥

I shape my destiny with the choices I make.

♥

My beauty is radiant, both inside and out.

♥

Every day, I become a better version of myself.

♥

My mental health is a priority, and I nurture it with positivity.

♥

I am not afraid to stand out and embrace my uniqueness.

♥

I speak words of love and kindness to myself daily.

♥

My future is as bright as the dreams I dare to dream.

♥

The world is better with me in it.

♥

I am filled with joy, purpose, and determination.

♥

My skin sparkles like gold; it is an incredible shade of brown.

♥

I am an important member of my family.

♥

I am not to blame for being bullied.

♥

Someone else's opinion of me does not define me.

♥

I am deserving of love, respect, and kindness.

♥

I am stronger than the words and actions of bullies.

♥

I am important.

♥

I am a valued member of my family.

♥

Every challenge I face makes me stronger and more resilient.

♥

I have the power within me to rise above negativity.

♥

I love and accept myself just as I am.

♥

I am worthy of all the good things that come my way.

♥

I have a unique light inside of me that shines brightly.

♥

Bullying does not determine my worth; I know who I truly am.

♥

I am surrounded by love, even if I can't see it right now.

♥

Just because other people say something does not mean it is true.

♥

I am better than the rest.

♥

I work hard; very hard.

♥

It is OK to listen to my heart and trust my better judgment.

♥

No one can stop me when I decide to do something.

♥

I am proud of who I am; no one can take that away from me.

♥

I am allowed to voice my feelings and stand up for myself.

♥

I believe in myself and in what I am capable of doing.

♥

I am smart, clever, and always open to learning.

♥

My strength helps me to overcome adversity.

♥

My family and friends love and support me.

♥

It's OK to feel proud of my accomplishments.

♥

I am allowed to listen to my heart and trust my judgment.

♥

My feelings and thoughts are valid and worthy.

♥

I deserve happiness, contentment, and joy.

♥

I am brighter than the brightest star in the sky.

♥

I am making smart decisions for myself, and it feels good.

♥

I am amazing!

♥

The things that make me different are what define the real me.

♥

I will not compare myself to people on the internet.

♥

When I fall down, I immediately get back up.

♥

I know the value of being a good listener.

♥

I believe in myself both inside and out.

♥

My opinion matters and is valuable.

♥

My dreams are within reach.

♥

Perfection is not a prerequisite for acceptance.

♥

I love and accept my body as it is.

♥

I am more than just my appearance; I am a complete person.

♥

Societal standards don't define my self-worth.

♥

My confidence is inspiring.

♥

I learn from my mistakes.

♥

I am my only limit.

♥

I am caring to others.

♥

Before I was born, I was prayed for and hoped for.

♥

Nothing can steal my joy.

♥

I have a powerful voice.

♥

My brown skin is beautiful, and it even absorbs sunlight!

♥

I am becoming healthier each and every day.

♥

I will learn from yesterday and live for today.

♥

I am the expert when it comes to my own experience and identity.

♥

I am proud to be Black.

♥

I lead by example and don't allow others to take me off course.

♥

I am capable of learning and achieving greatness.

♥

I embrace challenges as opportunities to grow.

♥

I am true to myself, regardless of what others think.

♥

I confidently express my individuality.

♥

I surround myself with positive and supportive friends.

♥

I acknowledge and honor all my emotions.

♥

I am deserving of love, happiness, and peace.

♥

I shine brighter than everyone else in the room.

♥

I only compare myself to myself.

♥

I let go of things and thoughts that no longer serve me.

♥

I rise above negativity and choose positivity.

♥

I am brave and stand up for what I believe in.

♥

I am resilient, and any challenge I face is an opportunity to grow stronger.

♥

I am carefully planning my future, and it is going to be fulfilling.

♥

I am coachable, and I readily seek out and accept good advice.

♥

I deserve to move through life with ease.

♥

I reject societal standards that don't align with me.

♥

I am allowed to be myself and show people who I am.

♥

I allow people to show up for me.

♥

I am loving, loved, and lovable.

♥

I attract genuine friendships with people who want the best for me.

♥

My connections with others are steeped in good intentions.

♥

The love I have for myself increases my capacity to love others.

♥

I am always headed in the right direction.

♥

By shining my light, I help others shine theirs.

♥

I don't have to earn my worth.

♥

I belong in any space I walk into.

♥

I focus on what gives me energy. My energy serves as my compass.

♥

Being me is how I win.

♥

I am my best source of inspiration.

♥

I am loved and supported.

♥

I know social media is primarily fake, and I will not allow staged posts to make me feel bad about myself and my life.

♥

My life is just beginning, and my future is bright.

♥

My self-worth is high.

♥

I am the best version of myself, just as I am.

♥

I am unconditionally worthy.

♥

My magic speaks for itself.

♥

I am stepping into my power.

♥

I release what doesn't reciprocate my energy.

♥

I trust the timing of my life.

♥

I am energetically aligned with all I desire.

♥

I find small ways to receive each day.

♥

My greatest glow-up is internal.

♥

I manifest things as they should be, not as I want them.

♥

I honor my commitment to take care of myself.

♥

I move my body in ways that bring me joy.

♥

The chaos around me is no match for the calmness within me.

♥

I inhale my hopes and dreams and exhale my fears.

♥

I release what doesn't reciprocate my energy.

♥

I find peace through discipline.

♥

I am becoming a better version of myself each day.

♥

My energy is palpable when I walk into a room.

♥

How others perceive me doesn't define me.

♥

I have everything to gain by releasing the grip of shame.

♥

By acknowledging my inner child, I am one step closer to healing.

♥

I accept radical responsibility for creating my dream life.

♥

My heart and mind are open and ready for new experiences.

♥

I achieve my goals by focusing on one at a time.

♥

I tap into my magic by trusting my intuition.

♥

I am safe and loved by my friends and family.

♥

I will not compare myself to people on the internet.

♥

I do my best not to engage in negative self-talk; instead, I use positive self-talk to feel better.

♥

My actions match my goals.

♥

I attract what I want by being what I want.

♥

I love that I am determined and never give up.

♥

I have such a big heart!

♥

I have a tremendous sense of humor.

♥

I am proud of how my mind works.

♥

I love spending time with people who respect me.

♥

I will not spend time with people who do not respect me.

♥

I make the world a better place.

♥

I love my friends, my family, and my community.

♥

Everything will work out; just breathe.

♥

My voice matters and is valued.

♥

People enjoy spending time with me.

♥

I accept myself for who I am.

♥

I am building my future.

♥

My happiness is up to me.

♥

My self-worth is high. I am the best version of myself just as I am.

♥

I radiate positive energy.

♥

Wonderful things are going to happen to me.

♥

With every breath, I feel stronger.

♥

I will never lessen my standards for anyone.

♥

I'll never give anyone the right or strength to demolish my self-esteem.

♥

I am a desirable and attractive black person.

♥

I acknowledge myself as deserving of love and respect.

♥

People with white skin spend hours laying in the sun trying to get my beautiful brown skin; I am lucky and was born with this beautiful skin.

♥

I maintain my dignity while speaking and presenting my views.

♥

I am a boss.

♥

I encircle myself with different powerful and bright people.

♥

I have the power to accomplish my goals.

♥

I face challenges with resilience and strength.

♥

I act with courage and confidence.

♥

I face trials and challenges head-on.

♥

I am capable and worthy of success.

♥

I am worthy of a fantastic partnership.

♥

I am a blessing to those around me.

♥

I feel free to express my emotions.

♥

I don't have to be strong at all times.

♥

I am worthy of love and belonging.

♥

My vulnerability is a strength.

♥

I am proud of the man I am becoming.

♥

I am valued in my work, home, and community.

♥

I am committed to being my best self.

♥

I don't need to be perfect to be accepted.

♥

It is a privilege to get to know the true me.

♥

My body is my home, and I will treat it with care.

♥

I can become anything I want if I put my heart into it.

♥

I am capable of so much, constantly surprising myself with my abilities.

♥

I am unstoppable, moving forward no matter the obstacles.

♥

I am loved, cherished, and appreciated by those around me.

♥

I respect and honor my roots, embracing the beauty of my heritage.

♥

I spread love, understanding, and positivity wherever I go.

♥

I have a powerful voice, and it deserves to be heard.

♥

My mind is filled with knowledge, wisdom, and creativity.

♥

I lead, guiding others with respect, honesty, and purpose.

♥

My brown skin is beautiful and rich and tells a story.

♥

Every day, I become better, stronger, and more resilient.

♥

I am strong, facing challenges with courage and determination.

♥

I deserve respect, love, and all the good things life offers.

♥

I am unique; no one in the world is quite like me.

♥

My hair is the perfect crown, symbolizing my strength and beauty.

♥

I am destined for greatness, and nothing can hold me back.

♥

My lips, nose, and other features are all beautiful expressions of
my heritage.

♥

I am in charge of my destiny, shaping my path with my choices.

♥

I am confident and believe in my abilities and values.

♥

I come from a strong Black family that guides and supports me.

♥

I know that a true friend lifts me up and never tries to tear me down.

♥

I am a warrior; I will not tolerate those who treat me with disrespect.

♥

I only do things that make me feel good about myself; I will not engage in toxic behaviors.

♥

I can handle challenging situations.

♥

I bravely strive to better myself.

♥

I am in touch with my emotions.

♥

My emotions are worthy.

♥

I love myself.

♥

I am resilient.

♥

I can change my thoughts.

I can't control others.

I can ask for help when I need it.

I am an asset to my school.

I know things will not always go as planned, and that is OK; I will adapt.

I'm grateful for everything in my life.

Setbacks are an opportunity for growth.

♥

I am confident in my goals and work towards them each day.

♥

I walk into every room with confidence and self-assurance.

♥

My goals and dreams are valid and meaningful.

♥

I am humble and learn from my mistakes.

♥

I have a lot to offer in my relationships.

♥

I embrace the joys and messiness of learning how to be my best self.

♥

I am a good family member.

I am allowed to be imperfect and make mistakes.

I strive every day to be a good role model.

I am willing to learn and grow as I mature.

I am proud of my cultural heritage.

I am kind, and I assist those who require my assistance.

I enjoy taking time just for myself, and it is OK.

♥

I am high-spirited and fearless.

♥

I am proud of my capabilities.

♥

I will ensure that people around me feel safe and secure.

♥

I perform my duties with utmost sincerity and dedication.

♥

I do not make other people feel insecure about their shortcomings.

♥

I do not waste my time with or on the haters.

♥

I attract affluent and successful people into my life.

♥

I have trust in myself.

♥

I maintain my dignity while speaking and presenting my views.

♥

I understand that my activities become a pattern of life, so I will constantly do the appropriate things.

♥

I always choose to take the high road.

♥

I only compare myself to myself.

♥

It is enough to do my best.

♥

I know that taking care of myself is very important and healthy.

♥

I am an upstander, not a bystander.

♥

I know there will be hard days and challenging moments, they are a part of life, and I will survive them.

♥

I have the strength to move past this and thrive.

♥

My worth is determined by how I treat myself, not how others treat me.

♥

I prioritize my peace and maintaining my composure.

♥

I have the right to a safe and respectful environment.

♥

I have overcome challenges before, and I can overcome this too.

♥

Every day, I grow stronger and more confident in who I am.

♥

I deserve friendships that uplift, support, and respect me.

♥

My experiences shape me but do not define me.

♥

I am deserving of love, understanding, and compassion.

♥

I will not let the actions of others dim my shine.

♥

I have a bright future ahead of me beyond this moment.

♥

I am grateful for my beauty.

♥

I am surrounded by people who see my value and worth.

♥

I feel sorry for people who pick on other people.

♥

Being me is how I win. I am my best source of inspiration.

♥

My energy serves as my compass. I am unconditionally worthy.

♥

I am stepping into my power. My greatest glow-up is internal.

♥

I am loved and supported.

♥

Being me is how I win.

♥

I am a great person.

♥

I belong in any space I walk into.

♥

I am the best version of myself just as I am.

♥

My black community supports me and wants the best for me.

♥

I trust the timing of my life.

♥

I am a valued member of my school.

♥

I manifest things as they should be, not as I want them.

♥

I am a strong, capable student. I see you growing and making progress.

♥

My body is beautifully perfect. It is the ideal body for me.

♥

I am a magnet for blessings.

♥

Mistakes are not the end of you. You are resilient and powerful.

♥

My hair is the perfect halo for my head. It's stunning and strong and soft, just like you.

♥

My future is my own. You will have everything you need to become the woman you're supposed to be.

♥

I don't need all the answers to remain grounded in this moment.

♥

I am stepping into my power.

♥

I walk through my school with my head held high because I am a strong, beautiful black young person.

♥

I honor my commitment to take care of myself.

♥

I move my body in ways that bring me joy.

♥

I am gentle with myself through all transitions.

♥

I inhale my dreams and exhale my fears.

♥

I know that people who are prejudiced against me are sad on the inside and feel threatened by my beautiful skin and amazing soul.

♥

Rest is a top priority for me.

♥

I am uniquely gifted. No one else can do exactly what I do precisely the way I do it.

♥

Even on challenging days, I remember I am resilient, powerful, and can learn from any situation.

♥

I am a good and loyal friend; I care deeply about my friends.

♥

I am proud of who I am and embrace my rich Black heritage daily.

♥

I am destined for greatness and have the power to shape my future.

♥

My hair is the perfect halo for my head, reflecting strength, beauty, and softness.

♥

I grow better daily, harnessing the power of positivity and love.

♥

I light up the world with my radiant smile and powerful voice.

♥

Challenges do not define me. I am strong, capable, and prepared for any opportunity that comes my way.

♥

I can find humor in the day-to-day.

♥

I only compare myself to myself.

♥

I can't control other people but I can control how I respond to them.

♥

I am a fighter who doesn't give up.

♥

I am honest and trustworthy.

♥

I am not affected by racial slurs; I know that people who use racial slurs are not very intelligent and are leading sad lives.

♥

I believe in myself, trust in my decisions, and am inspired by the limitless possibilities of the future.

♥

My confidence shines bright, inspiring others around me.

♥

I am the master of my destiny, filled with joy, love, and positivity.

♥

The world needs me. My ideas, voice, and spirit contribute to making it a better place.

♥

I am unstoppable.

♥

I value kindness, appreciate those who show me compassion, and always try to be kind to others.

♥

I know that failing at a task means I am one step closer to figuring out how to do it.

♥

I am not just my grades or achievements. I am a beacon of growth, progress, and endless potential.

♥

My heart and mind are open, guiding me with wisdom and love in every decision I make.

♥

I am a beacon of hope for my community, embodying leadership and making my ancestors proud.

♥

I embrace every new day with gratitude, understanding the power of positivity in shaping my path.

♥

I have the strength and bravery to stand out, to make a difference, and to be the change I wish to see in the world.

♥

I am kind, thoughtful, and generous, always seeking to uplift those around me.

♥

I am unstoppable, fueled by passion, creativity, and the knowledge that I can achieve anything I set my mind to.

♥

I am surrounded by love from my family, community, and, most importantly, from within.

♥

I am the only person who can decide how I feel, and I choose to feel powerful.

♥

I smile when people try to cut me down; it just means they know
I am better than them and feel intimidated by me.

♥

I am uniquely gifted. No one else in the world can do exactly what
I do in precisely the way I do it. I am amazing.

♥

I am healthy. My mind is healthy. My spirit is healthy. My heart
is healthy. My body is healthy. Because I am healthy, I am whole.
Because I am whole, I am prepared for anything and everything.

♥

I can and will achieve anything I set my mind to.

♥

I am an asset to our community.

♥

I have leadership qualities.

♥

I make our people and our ancestors proud.

♥

I am a giving, generous person.

♥

I am open-hearted and wise.

♥

I am a magnet for blessings.

♥

My hair is the perfect halo for my head. It's stunning and strong
and soft at the same time, just like me.

♥

My future is my own. I will have everything I need to become the
person I am supposed to be.

♥

I light the world with my smile.

♥

I have a powerful voice.

♥

My mind is filled with knowledge.

♥

I am exceptional.

♥

I am creative.

♥

I am thoughtful.

♥

I can do hard things.

♥

I am not afraid to stand out.

♥

I speak kindly to myself.

♥

My future is bright.

♥

The world needs me.

♥

I am capable.

♥

I am constantly growing, learning, and expanding my intellect.

♥

Every challenge I face is an opportunity to showcase my intelligence.

♥

With every lesson, I am becoming the best version of myself.

♥

I trust in my wisdom and my ability to make informed decisions.

♥

I am a beacon of knowledge, and my light shines bright.

♥

Every test I face is a testament to my resilience and intellect.

♥

I believe in my skills, talents, and the vast knowledge I possess.

♥

I deserve all the academic achievements and honors that come my way.

♥

With passion and intelligence, I am paving my path to success.

♥

Every day in school, I prove to myself just how smart I am.

♥

I embrace new challenges because they make me stronger and wiser.

♥

My potential is limitless, and my intelligence knows no bounds.

♥

I am proud of my intellect and the unique perspective I bring.

♥

The world recognizes and respects my intelligence and capabilities.

♥

I am surrounded by opportunities to showcase my knowledge and skills.

♥

Every study session, every class, is a step closer to my academic goals.

♥

I am shaping my future with the power of my intelligence.

♥

My mind is a treasure trove of knowledge, and I am proud of it.

♥

I am confident in my abilities and the knowledge I've gained in
school.

♥

I approach every situation with an open mind and a thirst for
knowledge.

♥

I am making a difference in the world with my intelligence and
skills.

♥

Every accomplishment in school is a reflection of my hard work
and intelligence.

♥

I am a young woman of substance, intellect, and immense potential.

♥

I believe in myself and my abilities.

♥

I expect the best for myself and will accept nothing less.

♥

I am valued just as I am.

♥

I am capable of accomplishing anything I put my mind to.

♥

I uplift the people around me.

♥

I deserve abundance in all parts of my life.

♥

I am worthy of love, respect, and all the happiness in the world.

♥

Some people lay out in the sun for hours, trying to get their pale skin to look as golden and beautiful as mine.

♥

My love and compassion create harmony in my life.

♥

I practice kindness toward myself and others.

♥

I am grateful for the changing of the seasons and the changes in my life.

♥

I am in tune with my innermost feelings.

♥

I am comfortable with who I am.

♥

Health, wealth, and harmony are entering my life.

♥

I am a valuable person.

♥

My inner strength is invincible.

♥

I commit myself entirely to feeling good.

♥

I am full of confidence, and everyone around me can feel that.

♥

My happiness is up to me.

♥

I am ready and open to receiving good things in my life.

♥

Courage accompanies me everywhere I go.

♥

I communicate with ease and confidence.

♥

I am my best source of motivation.

♥

I acknowledge my self-worth.

♥

Being confident comes naturally to me.

♥

I am full of energy and optimism. I am ready to find joy.

♥

I can overcome negative thoughts and situations. I choose positive!

♥

I have been given many talents. Today I will use them.

♥

I possess the qualities I need to be successful.

♥

Today I am thankful for new experiences.

♥

I will honor my need to rest and recharge.

♥

I choose to live in a way that brings peace, joy, and happiness to myself and others.

♥

Today is the beginning of whatever I want.

♥

My body deserves to be cared for, so I feed it nourishing food and energizing exercise.

♥

I have the power to change my story.

♥

I replace any negative thoughts that come to my mind with strong, powerful positive thoughts.

♥

I am a young queen, strong and courageous.

♥

I am destined to achieve great things.

♥

I am beautiful, inside and out.

♥

Today I will spread positivity.

♥

My mind is incredible; my imagination knows no bounds; no one can limit me.

♥

My voice matters, and my words carry weight.

♥

I am proud of my rich heritage and culture.

♥

Every day, I grow wiser, kinder, and more compassionate.

♥

My hair is a crown that I wear with pride.

♥

It's OK to make mistakes.

♥

I am a great learner, capable of achieving anything I set my mind
to.

♥

I have the power to create a positive impact in my world.

♥

I am loved, valued, and respected.

♥

My skin is radiant and beautiful, reflecting the strength of my ancestors.

♥

I have the right to express myself freely and be heard.

♥

My dreams are valid and achievable.

♥

I am the author of my own story.

♥

I know that when other kids are mean to me, it has nothing to do with me; it just means they are sad and jealous of me.

♥

I am kind, generous, and always ready to share.

♥

I am a leader who guides others with integrity.

♥

I am resilient; every challenge I face makes me stronger.

♥

I am resourceful, and I will overcome this challenge

♥

I am not defined by my mistakes but by how I learn and grow from them.

♥

Every day is a new opportunity to be the best version of myself.

♥

I am valuable, and my worth is immeasurable.

I light the world with my smile.

My mind is filled with knowledge and wisdom.

I am incredibly special and unique.

I am comfortable taking control of situations, and others look up to me.

I make good choices that benefit me and those around me.

I deserve love and kindness, always.

♥

My confidence is inspiring to others.

♥

I believe in myself and my abilities.

♥

I am creative and full of original ideas.

♥

I am thoughtful and considerate of others.

♥

I trust myself and my instincts.

♥

I make a positive difference in my community.

♥

I am worthy of all the good things life has to offer.

♥

Today is a new day and a new opportunity for growth.

♥

I am in charge of my destiny, and I choose happiness.

♥

I deserve respect, and I respect others.

♥

I am destined for greatness.

♥

I am brave and courageous in all situations.

♥

I am beautiful, inside and out.

♥

I deserve good things and positivity in my life.

♥

I am kind and empathetic to others.

♥

I know the power of positive thinking, and I will apply it.

♥

I can do hard things and overcome any challenge that comes my way.

♥

My mind's ability to learn and remember is increasing every day.

♥

I am worthy of the best.

♥

I have a sharp mind which makes me an outstanding student.

♥

I feel thankful to be a student, and it shows.

♥

I radiate positive energy.

♥

I am a gifted student, and I can achieve anything.

♥

I love my student life!

♥

I embrace life as a student.

♥

My mind absorbs and processes new information with great speed.

♥

I am capable.

♥

I create a healthy balance in my life.

♥

There is no one better to be than me.

♥

I forgive myself for my mistakes.

♥

My ancestors paved the way for my peaceful existence.

♥

Today is going to be a great day.

♥

I have courage and confidence.

♥

I can control my happiness.

♥

I stand up for what I believe in.

♥

It's OK not to know everything.

♥

Today I choose to think positively.

♥

I can do tough things.

♥

I am proud of myself.

♥

I am free to make my own choices.

♥

I believe in myself and my abilities.

♥

Today, I will work through my challenges.

♥

I am whole.

♥

I can do anything.

♥

I am a decisive decision-maker and an excellent problem-solver.

♥

My skin shimmers and glows and is very healthy.

♥

I am intelligent, capable, and destined for greatness.

♥

I am constantly evolving, and my intelligence is crucial to my growth.

♥

I have unlimited potential within me.

♥

I am beautiful inside and out, deserving of respect, love, and all of
the good things in life.

♥

My mind is full of knowledge.

♥

I do not judge others by the color of their skin.

♥

I am proud to be me.

♥

I know my value, I will not engage with people who do not value
me.

♥

Every day, I am learning, growing, and becoming the best version
of myself.

♥

I know killing them with kindness is better than sinking to their level.

♥

People underestimate me; shame on them.

♥

My mental health matters.

♥

My journey is unique, and I am ideally suited for my path.

♥

I am a beacon of positivity, attracting blessings, opportunities, and joy into my life.

♥

I am proud of myself and my accomplishments.

❤

Many exciting experiences await me.

❤

Mistakes help me to learn and grow.

❤

Anything is possible.

❤

I radiate positive energy.

❤

I am smart.

❤

My intellect and work ethic can help me achieve my dreams in
school and beyond.

Thank You

Hello, I hope you have enjoyed these affirmations.

Many readers are unaware of how difficult it is to get reviews and how much they help authors like me.

I would greatly appreciate it if you could support me and help get the word out to other people about this book.

It is easy to leave a review, and I greatly appreciate every single review.

To leave a review, please either go to this link or scan this QR code. I am very grateful for your support.

https://amzn.to/462e0OO

References

References

- Be Happy Human. (n.d.). Affirmations for men. Retrieved August 13, 2023, from https://behappyhuman.com/affirmations-for-men/.

- Gratefulness.me. (n.d.). Positive affirmations for kids. Retrieved August 13, 2023, from https://blog.gratefulness.me/positive-affirmations-for-kids/.

- Gratefulness.me. (n.d.). 20 affirmations to say to yourself when you need support. Retrieved August 13, 2023, from https://blog.gratefulness.me/20-affirmations-to-say-to-yourself-when-you-need-support/.

- Balanced Black Girl. (n.d.). 10 affirmations guide glow up. Retrieved August 13, 2023, from https://www.balancedblackgirl.com/10-affirmations-guide-glow-up/.

- Happier Human. (n.d.). Positive affirmations for teens. Retrieved August 13, 2023, from https://www.happier human.com/positive-affirmations-teens/.

- Living Well Mom. (n.d.). Positive affirmations for teens. Retrieved August 13, 2023, from https://livingwellmo m.com/positive-affirmations-for-teens/.

- Lyn Loves. (n.d.). Positive affirmations for black children. Retrieved August 13, 2023, from https://lynloves.com/ positive-affirmations-for-black-children/.

- MentalHelp.net. (n.d.). 140 daily positive affirmations for men. Retrieved August 13, 2023, from https://www.mentalhelp.net/blogs/140-daily-pos itive-affirmations-for-men/.

- New Horizon Academy. (n.d.). 20 positive affirmations remind child loved. Retrieved August 13, 2023, from https://www.newhorizonacademy.net/20-positiv e-affirmations-remind-child-loved/.

- NPR. (2022, February 26). Reflecting on the power of affirmations for Black History Month. Retrieved August 13, 2023, from https://www.npr.org/sections/pictureshow/2022/02/26 /1080104890/reflecting-on-the-power-of-affirmations-f or-black-history-month.

- Our West Nest. (n.d.). Morning affirmations and quotes

for black women to empower themselves. Retrieved August 13, 2023, from https://www.ourwestnest.com/blogposts/2020/11/30/morning-affirmations-and-quotes-for-black-women-to-empower-themselves.

- Our West Nest. (n.d.). Positive affirmations for black kids. Retrieved August 13, 2023, from https://www.ourwestnest.com/blogposts/0/0/6/positive-affirmations-for-black-kids.

- Parents with Confidence. (n.d.). 125 positive affirmations for kids to skyrocket strength, confidence, and self-love. Retrieved August 13, 2023, from https://parentswithconfidence.com/125-positive-affirmations-for-kids-to-skyrocket-strength-confidence-and-self-love/.

- Prodigy Game. (n.d.). Positive affirmations for kids. Retrieved August 13, 2023, from https://www.prodigygame.com/main-en/blog/positive-affirmations-for-kids/.

Positive Affirmations for Black Kids Volume 2

Thoughtful Affirmations Designed to
Increase Self-Confidence, Instill Self-Esteem,
Grow Resilience, and Encourage Self-Love.
Volume 2

Nia Simone

Dedication

This book would not be possible without the love and support of
T and P.

Contents

Introduction

Did you know every word, every thought, and every sentence you think and say aloud holds great power? Your words and thoughts are powerful, and they influence how you feel about yourself, how you see yourself, and how you project yourself to others. Fill your mind and body with nurturing, supportive thoughts, and cast away any negative thoughts that might creep in. This book is a collection of affirmations designed to honor your strength, brilliance, and boundless potential. These carefully crafted affirmations are for you, the black child who is both a promise to the future and a testament to a rich legacy that runs deep with history, culture, and accomplishment.

In the pages that follow, you will find affirmations that speak to the heart of who you are and who you will become. These affirmations are more than just sentences; they are seeds. When planted in the fertile soil of your young mind, they have the power to bloom into forests of confidence, self-love, and a strong sense of self-worth that will stand tall against any storm.

For too long, many voices in the world have spun narratives that don't reflect the fullness of your beauty, the depth of your capability, or the height of your dreams. This book aims to change that by being a mirror to show you your true reflection—a reflection of someone who is powerful, good, and worthy of all the good that life has to offer.

As you hear and repeat these words, you will embark on a journey of affirmation. An affirmation is a positive statement that can help you to challenge and overcome self-sabotaging and negative thoughts. When you repeat them often, and believe in them, you can start to make positive changes in your life. It is a simple yet very profound act of self-empowerment.

Let these affirmations teach you to embrace the language of self-love and resilience. They are like the sun that warms the earth: essential for growth. For black children, these affirmations are rays of light, guiding your path with hope and pride in who you are. They serve as a constant reminder that you are not defined by stereotypes or by the challenges you face but by the limitless potential and goodness within you.

This collection of affirmations is designed with you in mind—to lift you up when you feel down, to help you see how smart, creative, kind, and capable you are, even if others fail to see it. With every "I am" and "I can," you are declaring your place in the world, taking ownership of your story, and shaping your destiny with intention and power.

Self-esteem is the armor you'll wear on your journey through childhood and beyond. It will help you face any challenge, embrace your individuality, and recognize the strength you have to rise above any obstacle. Self-confidence is your compass, helping you navigate through life's complexities with a sense of assurance and poise. This audiobook is here to nurture those qualities in you so that you can walk into any room knowing your value does not diminish because of others' inability to see it.

Remember, feeling good about yourself is your right, and it is the foundation from which you can reach for the stars. This book is a daily reminder that you are not alone in your journey. Each page is a friend, a mentor, and a cheerleader, urging you to see the beauty in your melanin, the power in your heritage, and the brilliance in your mind. It's a celebration of the skin you're in, the curl of your hair, the sound of your voice, and the genius of your thoughts.

As you read and repeat these affirmations, picture them as your allies in crafting the story of 'You'—a story that is as expansive as the universe and as unique as your fingerprint. Let these words be the daily bread for your soul, nourishing and strengthening you with each passing day.

This book also stands as a bridge between generations. For parents and guardians, it is a way to engage with young ones, fostering a dialogue that affirms and supports their growth and well-being. For educators and mentors, it is a resource to encourage and inspire, to build a classroom environment that is inclusive and celebratory of every child's identity and potential.

We invite you, the parents, the guardians, the teachers, and the mentors, to use this book as a conversation starter and a learning tool. Engage with these affirmations together with your children. Encourage them to speak these words out loud, to write them down, and to live them. Help them understand the power that resides in their speech and the transformative effect it can have on their reality.

With every affirmation, you will not only be learning new words but also weaving a protective garment for your psyche, one that will repel the cold of doubt and the rain of negativity. This garment will grow with you, adapting and expanding to your ever-evolving story.

This is your book, your mantra, and your magic. Let it both protect you from harm and guide you toward your truest expression of self. You are the protagonist of an epic tale, and as you narrate your journey with these affirmations, remember that you are writing chapters that future generations will read with pride.

Embrace this journey, for it is yours alone—beautiful, bold, and bright. And let these affirmations be the wings upon which you will soar to your destiny.

I recommend that you do your best to make time every day to read and repeat a portion of these affirmations. The best times are first thing in the morning and last thing in the evening before you go to bed. But anytime you can find is just perfect.

Affirmations

Every part of me is a friend I love and understand.

♥

I am strong, capable, and ready to shine.

♥

I celebrate my uniqueness; it's my signature in the world.

♥

My smile is my crown, and I wear it proudly every day.

♥

I am more than a number on a scale; I am full of wonders.

♥

Kindness is my shield, and confidence is my sword.

♥

I am the author of my story, and it's a bestseller.

♥

I build my dreams with the power of my positive thoughts.

♥

I am a masterpiece, perfectly crafted and endlessly loved.

♥

Every step I take is a dance of my own making.

♥

My worth is immeasurable, and my potential is limitless.

♥

Challenges make me stronger and braver.

♥

I am wrapped in courage, tied with wit, and adorned with wisdom.

♥

I am a treasure chest of talents waiting to be explored.

♥

My heart is full of joy that spills into the world.

♥

I am a loyal and caring friend.

♥

I know right from wrong.

♥

I have the power to change the world with my kindness.

♥

Every day, in every way, I am getting stronger.

♥

I am a brilliant student of life, learning and growing every day.

♥

I am an ocean of possibilities, deep and vast.

♥

I have a voice that echoes with the strength of my spirit.

♥

My laughter adds light to the world and joy to my heart.

♥

I respect my body as the amazing companion that it is.

💛

I am a rainbow of possibilities, colorful and bright.

💛

I love myself deeply, truly, and unconditionally.

💛

I am proud of my beautiful skin, just as it is.

💛

My hair is a crown of glory and strength.

💛

I am rooted in the rich soil of history and heritage.

💛

My ancestors' dreams live and breathe in me.

♥

I am the embodiment of resilience and excellence.

♥

My voice carries the wisdom of generations.

♥

I am in control of my emotional well-being.

♥

I walk in the light of those who paved the way for me.

♥

My laughter is a song of freedom and joy.

♥

I am sculpted in the image of greatness.

♥

My potential is boundless, and my ambitions are lofty.

♥

I embrace the magic in my melanin and shine brightly.

♥

I honor my culture by being my authentic self.

♥

My uniqueness is a gift to the world.

♥

I am woven from a fabric of stars and limitless possibilities.

♥

I am a vessel of love and a beacon of hope.

♥

The strength of my will is forged by the fire of determination.

♥

I am a living legacy, a bridge to the future.

♥

I do the hard work that others can't do.

♥

I am fueled by the courage of my convictions.

♥

My heart is a fortress, and my spirit is invincible.

♥

I am surrounded by a community that lifts me higher.

♥

The richness of my heritage is a testament to my inner strength.

♥

My intelligence is a torch that lights the path forward.

♥

I speak my truth with confidence and clarity.

♥

I am the pride of my ancestors and the promise of tomorrow.

♥

I am loved, valued, and filled with the power to make a difference.

♥

I am a beautiful story in the making.

♥

My mind is a garden where big dreams grow.

♥

I am brave, strong, and smart in every way.

♥

My skin is a shade of awesome.

♥

I am loved for who I am, just as I am.

♥

My voice is important, and my words matter.

♥

I am a creator of happiness and a dreamer of big dreams.

♥

Every day, I am learning and getting better.

♥

I stand tall like the kings and queens of my heritage.

♥

I am a bright star in a vast sky.

♥

My smile brings joy to the world.

♥

I am full of ideas that can change the world.

♥

I am worthy of respect and kindness.

♥

My laughter is a sign of my inner strength.

♥

I can achieve anything with effort and determination.

♥

I am a leader of tomorrow.

♥

I am a learner today and a teacher tomorrow.

♥

My possibilities are endless.

♥

I am a living legacy of resilience and grace.

♥

I love the uniqueness that is me.

♥

I embrace the challenges that make me grow.

♥

I am an explorer in the world of knowledge.

♥

I am a vessel of peace and understanding.

♥

I am a joyful celebration of black beauty.

♥

You can only achieve success after many failures.

♥

My confidence shines from within me.

♥

I respect my roots and grow towards my future.

♥

I am not just a number, I am a story unfolding.

♥

My courage is like the lion, mighty and fearless.

♥

I am a tapestry of talent and tenacity.

♥

I embrace positive thoughts and banish negative thoughts.

♥

People look at me and see my confidence and my power.

♥

I respect myself, and others respect me too.

♥

I am a work of heart, creating my path with passion.

♥

I am respectful of elders and a role model for my peers.

♥

I bloom with the strength and warmth of the sun.

♥

I am an artwork painted with the colors of diversity and courage.

♥

My natural hair is a crown of beauty.

♥

I dance to the beat of my dreams.

♥

I am a harmonious melody in the symphony of life.

♥

I soar high on the wings of my aspirations.

♥

I am a river of hope, flowing toward my destiny.

♥

My mind is powerful and full of brilliant ideas.

♥

I am intelligent in a way that is uniquely mine.

♥

I have the wisdom of my ancestors guiding me.

♥

My thoughts create a wonderful impact on the world.

♥

I am a critical thinker and a problem-solver.

♥

I am gentle and kind, do not mistake that for weakness.

♥

I am curious about the world and always learning more.

♥

My potential to succeed is limitless.

♥

I am inventive and resourceful.

♥

I carry the history of a people who are strong and wise.

♥

My creativity is a gift to my community and the world.

♥

I am as smart as I am strong.

♥

Knowledge is my playground, and I play with enthusiasm.

♥

I honor my heritage with my pursuit of education.

♥

I am a natural leader who inspires others.

♥

I do not let negative and mean people into my inner circle.

♥

I excel in my studies because I am dedicated.

♥

My intelligence is a bridge to my future success.

♥

I am a trailblazer, making paths for others to follow.

♥

I am a scholar and a gentle heart.

♥

Every question I ask sharpens my mind.

♥

My eager mind is my greatest asset.

♥

My body is my superpower, and I am its hero.

♥

I am a vibrant thinker and a keen learner.

♥

I am confident in my ability to solve difficult problems.

♥

I have a rich cultural legacy that enhances my smarts.

♥

My learning grows deeper with every challenge I overcome.

♥

I am a beacon of innovation and originality.

♥

I am wise beyond my years and learning more every day.

♥

My intelligence is just one of my many amazing qualities.

♥

I respect the knowledge passed down through generations.

♥

I am capable of academic excellence.

♥

I am deserving of love and acceptance.

♥

I am proud of my intellectual achievements.

♥

I am a quick learner and a wise decision-maker.

♥

My thoughts and ideas are valuable and respected.

♥

I am destined for greatness in all my academic pursuits.

♥

I am equipped with the strength and determination to learn.

♥

My culture enriches my knowledge and understanding of the world.

♥

I cherish my unique perspective and share it proudly.

♥

I am an intellectual champion, winning through wisdom.

♥

My mind is an endless ocean of potential.

♥

I am a living legacy of intelligence and courage.

♥

I am a shining example of the power of education.

♥

I am a strong leader.

♥

I use my smarts to make positive changes in my community.

♥

I am the architect of my dreams and build them with knowledge.

♥

I am a visionary, seeing opportunities where others see obstacles.

♥

My voice carries the insight of a deep thinker.

♥

I deserve to be treated with respect.

♥

I embrace complex concepts with excitement and confidence.

♥

I am an eloquent speaker and a thoughtful listener.

♥

I challenge myself to reach new heights in my education.

♥

I celebrate my mind with every book I read and every question I ask.

♥

I am inspired by the great thinkers of my heritage and strive to honor them with my learning.

♥

My beauty shines from within me, bright and true.

♥

I am thoughtful, kind, and respectful.

♥

I am a dazzling blend of history, culture, and potential.

♥

My skin is a tapestry of strength and splendor.

♥

The beauty of my ancestors blooms within me.

♥

My imagination is great.

♥

I am a valuable member of my community with much to contribute.

♥

My life is a beautiful story that I am writing every day.

♥

I have the strength of my ancestors in me, guiding my way.

♥

I have a brilliant mind and a kind heart united in excellence.

♥

My voice is powerful and echoes with the wisdom of the ages.

♥

I have the power to achieve my goals, step by step, day by day.

♥

I am rooted in the love of those who came before me.

♥

My dreams are heard and supported by the universe.

♥

I am surrounded by a sky full of stars; I shine with them.

♥

I walk with confidence, knowing I am worthy of respect.

♥

The love in my heart is as deep as the ocean and as vast as the sky.

♥

My laughter is a song that brightens the world's melody.

♥

I am a courageous seeker of knowledge and truth.

♥

I am a diamond, precious and unbreakable.

♥

I contribute to class discussions with insightful comments.

♥

My skin is rich with history and radiant with potential.

♥

I am defining my future as a bright and brave leader.

♥

I honor my heritage and contribute to its story of strength.

♥

I am not a stereotype; I am an original masterpiece.

♥

My mind is a library of wisdom and imagination.

♥

I carry the courage of kings and queens in my heart.

♥

I am a force of love and positive change in the world.

♥

The content of my character is my truest measure.

♥

I am the architect of my dreams and the builder of my joy.

♥

My voice is a powerful instrument of truth and kindness.

♥

I rise above limitations to reveal my highest self.

♥

I am breaking barriers with my intelligence and grace.

♥

My abilities are limitless and not defined by others' views.

♥

I am the pride of my ancestors and the hope for the future.

♥

My potential to succeed is infinite and knows no bounds.

♥

I stand tall, honoring the greatness within me.

♥

I celebrate the excellence that runs through my veins.

♥

My confidence is unshaken by ignorance and hate.

♥

I am a reflection of beauty, talent, and resilience.

♥

I am empowered by challenges; they prepare me for greatness.

♥

Every day, I am inspired to create a legacy of success.

♥

I embrace my identity and shape it with purpose and passion.

♥

I am a beacon of creativity and a powerhouse of innovation.

♥

I lead with compassion, intelligence, and unwavering strength.

♥

I am surrounded by a universe of possibilities, and I claim them
with open arms.

♥

My presence is a testament to the beauty of diversity.

♥

I am resilient, turning every challenge into strength.

♥

I am a living legacy, flourishing with each new day.

♥

My hands are capable of building dreams into reality.

♥

I am a work of art, painted with the strokes of greatness and grace.

♥

I am filled with the fortitude and spirit of warriors.

♥

I am a gift to my community, and my potential is limitless.

♥

The rhythm of my steps announces my purpose to the world.

♥

I embrace my identity with pride and joy.

♥

I am a beacon of hope and an emblem of a bright future.

♥

My imagination is a canvas for inventing wonders.

♥

I am a beloved and capable child, growing stronger every day.

♥

I am a masterpiece created with love and purpose.

♥

My eyes carry the depth of stars and stories untold.

♥

I radiate confidence and grace with every step.

♥

The rhythm of my heritage dances in my smile.

♥

I am wrapped in the glow of my rich heritage.

♥

My hair weaves the tales of my glorious lineage.

♥

I carry the elegance of the earth in my being.

♥

I am a canvas of endless possibilities.

♥

My spirit is as captivating as my presence.

♥

I wear my history with pride and my future with hope.

♥

My laughter is a symphony that brightens the world.

♥

I am adorned with the resilience and brilliance of my people.

♥

My presence is a gift to the world, one that I share generously.

♥

I am a unique expression of universal beauty.

♥

My beauty is a story written by a thousand ancestors.

♥

I am a living celebration of all that is beautiful and diverse.

♥

I flourish like a rose in a garden of diversity.

♥

I am grateful for my family and friends.

♥

My skin is kissed by the sun, a hue of divine beauty.

♥

I am the creator of joy and the bearer of beauty.

♥

My beauty defies norms and sets its own standards.

♥

I am a carrier of hope and an emblem of loveliness.

♥

In every language in the world, my beauty speaks volumes.

♥

I reflect the beauty of the world back to it.

♥

I am a bearer of beauty, inside and out.

♥

I am determined and resilient.

♥

I can do anything I set my mind to.

♥

Every feature of mine tells a story worth celebrating.

♥

I am a tapestry woven with threads of grace and power.

♥

I embrace the beauty that comes naturally to me.

♥

I am an expression of divine design and earthly elegance.

♥

My smile is a breathtaking display of joy.

♥

I am crowned with the glory of the stars and the strength of mountains.

♥

I move through the world with a beauty that is innate and empowering.

♥

My essence is composed of harmonious beauty and profound strength.

♥

I am a treasure, cherished, and admired by those who know me.

♥

My beauty resonates with the courage and love of my people.

♥

I am sculpted in finesse, rich in culture, and full of life.

♥

My beauty is as boundless as the sky and as vast as the ocean.

♥

I lead by example.

♥

The melody of my heritage is sung through my beauty.

♥

I am a vision of creativity and the image of dreams realized.

♥

I am complete as I am, and my own company is joyful and suffi-
cient.

♥

I attract the right people into my life at the right time.

♥

My worth is not measured by the number of friends I have but by
the kindness I hold in my heart.

♥

I am open to making new friends, but I am also okay being on my
own.

♥

I am a good friend to myself, and that's a wonderful beginning.

♥

My uniqueness is my superpower, and it draws people toward me when the time is right.

♥

I am patient with myself as I find the right circle of friends.

♥

Every person I meet has the potential to become a friend.

♥

I am becoming more confident in myself every day, which makes me a magnet for true friendship.

♥

I add value to others' lives just by being me.

♥

I choose to embrace the adventures that come with meeting new people.

♥

I am worthy of friendship and give friendship uniquely.

♥

Being alone sometimes gives me strength and teaches me about myself.

♥

I have a lot to offer as a friend, even if I haven't met the right friends yet.

♥

My solo journey is just as enriching as one shared with others.

♥

I am building a relationship with myself that will be the foundation for all other relationships.

♥

I can be both a solitary wanderer and a loyal friend.

♥

Confidence grows in me with each new day.

♥

I am learning to love myself more, which helps others love and appreciate me too.

♥

I find friendship in various forms, and not just in people my age.

♥

I grow and learn independently, preparing myself for future friendships.

♥

I enjoy exploring my interests, which will lead me to friends with similar passions.

♥

My heart is always open to genuine connections, which I will find in due time.

♥

I am kind, I am loved, and I am enough as I am.

♥

I express my needs and feelings, which is a sign of true friendship with myself and others.

♥

I am confident in making friends, knowing it starts with a smile and hello.

♥

I celebrate the person I am becoming, and this draws others to me.

♥

My solitude is a space for creativity and self-discovery.

❤️

I trust the journey of life to bring me friendships that will enlighten and nurture me.

❤️

I am a friend to the world, and in turn, kindness finds its way back to me.

❤️

Each day, I see the beauty in myself that the world sees in me.

❤️

My uniqueness is my signature, and my beauty is its flourish.

❤️

I am a declaration of magnificence and a whisper of wonder.

❤️

I stand in the light of my truth, and my beauty shines brighter for it.

♥

I am an infusion of wisdom, warmth, and wonder.

♥

People enjoy being around me.

♥

My beauty is the light that never dims, even in the darkest times.

♥

I am as gorgeous as a sunrise and as mystic as the night sky.

♥

The beauty in me is a lifelong journey of self-love and acceptance.

♥

My mind is a wellspring of great ideas.

♥

I stand tall on the shoulders of giants.

♥

My heart is brave; my spirit is boundless.

♥

I am deserving of respect and kindness.

♥

My words echo the wisdom of my ancestors.

♥

I am a legacy of strength and pride.

♥

I choose to speak with love and act with courage.

♥

My potential is unlimited, and my talents are plenty.

♥

I am grounded in dignity and soaring in dreams.

♥

My laughter is a celebration of my heritage.

♥

I do not waste my time with the haters.

♥

I am a masterpiece painted with the colors of greatness.

♥

I have the power to create change in the world.

♥

My hands build the future with hope and skill.

♥

I am confident, capable, and cherished.

♥

I honor my history by being my best self.

♥

My life is a canvas, and every day I paint it with joy.

♥

I am wise, wonderful, and full of curiosity.

♥

My dreams are valid, and my ambitions are high.

♥

I am the pride of my family and a friend to many.

♥

I walk in the truth of my beauty and the rhythm of my culture.

♥

My presence is a gift to those around me.

♥

I am making healthy food choices.

♥

I carry the spirit of heroes within me.

♥

I have a voice that resonates with power and sincerity.

♥

My roots are deep; my resolve is steadfast.

♥

I am surrounded by a universe of opportunities.

♥

Every challenge I face makes me stronger.

♥

I am the future, bright and promising.

♥

I am a joy to behold and a force for good.

♥

My creativity brings new solutions to the world.

♥

I respect myself, and the world respects me.

♥

My skin is a shade of divine, my smile a burst of sunshine.

♥

I am not just learning; I am excelling.

♥

I honor my heart and follow my moral code.

♥

I am the sum of many victories and countless possibilities.

♥

My courage is my crown, and I wear it with elegance.

♥

I am a leader on the stage of my own life.

♥

My life is a story of triumph and happy discovery.

♥

I am rooted in respect and grown with love.

♥

My character is built with the strength of my conviction.

♥

I am a living legacy full of potential and grace.

♥

My ideas are innovations that the world awaits.

♥

I see every setback as a setup for a comeback.

♥

I am loved deeply and widely by those in my life.

♥

My success is not if, but when.

♥

I am carving a path for myself that is mine alone to travel.

♥

I fill every room with my light and positive energy.

♥

I am a powerful creator of my personal and community narrative.

♥

My soul is filled with the light of a thousand stars.

♥

Every day, I grow more into the leader I'm meant to be.

♥

I am sculpting a world of beauty with my actions and beliefs.

Thank You

I hope you have enjoyed these affirmations. I would love to hear your thoughts on this book.

Many readers are unaware of how difficult it is to get reviews and how much they help authors like me.

I would greatly appreciate it if you could support me and help get the word out to other people about this book.

To leave a review, please either click on the link below or scan the QR code with your phone. I am very grateful for your support.

https://amzn.to/40EyCLL

References

References

Be Happy Human. (n.d.). Affirmations for men. Retrieved August 13, 2023, from https://behappyhuman.com/affirmations-for-men/.

Gratefulness.me. (n.d.). Positive affirmations for kids. Retrieved August 13, 2023, from https://blog.gratefulness.me/positive-affirmations-for-kids/.

Balanced Black Girl. (n.d.). 10 affirmations guide glow up. Retrieved August 13, 2023, from https://www.balancedblackgirl.com/10-affirmations-guide-glow-up/.

Happier Human. (n.d.). Positive affirmations for teens. Retrieved August 13, 2023, from https://www.happierhuman.com/positive-affirmations-teens/.

Living Well Mom. (n.d.). Positive affirmations for teens. Retrieved August 13, 2023, from https://livingwellmom.com/positive-affirmations-for-teens/.

Lyn Loves. (n.d.). Positive affirmations for black children. Retrieved August 13, 2023, from https://lynloves.com/positive-affirmations-for-black-children/.

MentalHelp.net. (n.d.). 140 daily positive affirmations for men. Retrieved August 13, 2023, from https://www.mentalhelp.net/blogs/140-daily-positive-affirmations-for-men/.

NPR. (2022, February 26). Reflecting on the power of affirmations for Black History Month. Retrieved August 13, 2023, from https://www.npr.org/sections/pictureshow/2022/02/26/1080104890/reflecting-on-the-power-of-affirmations-for-black-history-month.

Our West Nest. (n.d.). Morning affirmations and quotes for black women to empower themselves. Retrieved August 13, 2023, from https://www.ourwestnest.com/blogposts/2020/11/30/morning-affirmations-and-quotes-for-black-women-to-empower-themselves.

Our West Nest. (n.d.). Positive affirmations for black kids. Retrieved August 13, 2023, from https://www.ourwestnest.com/blogposts/0/0/6/positive-affirmations-for-black-kids.

Parents with Confidence. (n.d.). 125 positive affirmations for kids to skyrocket strength, confidence, and self-love. Retrieved August 13, 2023, from https://parentswithconfidence.com/125-positive-affirmations-for-kids-to-skyrocket-strength-confidence-and-self-love/.

Prodigy Game. (n.d.). Positive affirmations for kids. Retrieved August 13, 2023, from https://www.prodigygame.com/main-en/blog/positive-affirmations-for-kids/.

www.ingramcontent.com/pod-product-compliance
Lightning Source LLC
Chambersburg PA
CBHW070707130626
46553CB00005B/1877